God's Majesty in Color and Word

God's Majesty in Color and Word

JULLIENA OKAH

Published by Tate Publishing & Enterprises, LLC
127 E. Trade Center Terrace | Mustang, Oklahoma 73064 USA
1.888.361.9473 | www.tatepublishing.com

Tate Publishing is committed to excellence in the publishing industry. The company reflects the philosophy established by the founders, based on Psalm 68:11,
"The Lord gave the word and great was the company of those who published it."

Cover design by Joseph Emnace
Interior design by Jomar Ouano

Published in the United States of America

ISBN: 978-1-62994-977-2
1. Biography & Autobiography / Personal Memoirs
2. Body, Mind & Spirit / Supernatural
13.12.12

Inspired by the words of God
to encourage others.

In the beginning was the Word, and the Word
was with God, and the Word was God.
The same was in the beginning with God.
All things were made by him; and without him
was not anything made that was made.
In him was life; and the life was the light of men.
And the light shineth in darkness; and the
darkness comprehended it not.

New Testament: John: 1-5 KJV

In the beginning God created the heaven
and the earth.
And the earth was without form, and void;
and darkness was upon the face of the deep.

And the Spirit of God moved
upon the face of waters.
And God said, Let there be light
and there was light.

And God saw the light, that it was good:
and God divided the light from the darkness.

Genesis 1:1-4 KJV

I am the one who made the earth and created
people to live on it.
With my hands I stretched out the heavens.
All the stars are at my command.
I will raise up Cyrus to fulfill my righteous
purpose, and I will guide his actions.

Isaiah 45:12-13 NLT

I alone am God, the First and the Last.
It was my hand that laid the foundations
of the earth, my right hand that spread out
the heavens above.
When I call out the stars, they all appear
in order.

Isaiah 48:12-13 NLT

"To whom will you compare me?
Who is my equal?"

Isaiah 40:25 NLT

I am the LORD: there is no other God........
I create the light and make the darkness.
I send good times and bad times.
I, the LORD, am the one who does these things.

Isaiah 45:5-7 NLT

I am the LORD your God,
who stirs up the sea, causing its waves to roar.
My name is the LORD of Heaven's Armies.
And I have put my words in your mouth
and hidden you safely in my hand.
I stretched out the sky like a canopy.

Isaiah 51:15-16 NLT

Who else has held the oceans in his hand?
Who has mesured off the heavens
with his fingures?
Who else knows the weight of the earth
or has weighed the mountains and hills
on a scale?

Isaiah 40:12 NLT

I am the LORD; that is my name!
I will not give my glory to anyone else,
nor share my praise with carved idols.

Isaiah 42:8 NLT

I am the LORD, the God of all the peoples
of the world.
Is anything too hard for me?"

Jeremiah 32:27 NLT

What sorrow awaits those who argue
with their Creator.
Does a clay pot argue with its maker?

Isaiah 45:9 NLT

I will teach you wisdom's ways
and lead you in straight paths.
When you walk, you won't be held back;
when you run, you won't stumble.
Take hold of my instructions; don't let them go.
Guard them, for they are the key to life.

Proverbs 4:11-13 NLT

I am the LORD your God,
who teaches you what is good for you
and leads you along the paths
you should follow.
Oh, that you had listened to my commands!
Then you would have had peace following like a
gentle river and righteousness rolling over you
like waves in the sea.

Isaiah 48:17-18 NLT

Trust in the LORD with all thine heart;
and lean not unto thine own understanding.
In all thy ways acknowledge him, and he shall
direct thy paths.
Be not wise in thine own eyes:
fear the LORD, and depart from evil.

Proverbs 3:5-7 KJV

"My thoughts are not your thoughts,
neither are your ways my ways, saith the LORD.
For as the heavens are higher than the earth,
so are my ways higher than your ways,
and my thoughts than your thoughts.

Isaiah 55:8-9 KJV

"For I know the plans I have for you,"
say the LORD.
"They are plans for good and not for
disaster, to give you a future and a hope."

Jeremiah 29:11 NLT

Look up into the heavens.
Who created all the stars?
He brings them out like an army,
one after another, calling each by its name.
Because of his great power and incomparable
strength, not a single one is missing.

Isaiah 40:26 NLT

He is to be feared above all gods.

Psalm 96:4 NLT

God created the heavens and earth
and put everything in place.
He made the world to be lived in,
not to be a place of empty chaos.

Isaiah 45:18 NLT

God made the earth by his power,
and he preserves it by his wisdom.
With his own understanding
he stretched out the heavens.
When he speaks in the thunder,
the heavens roar with rain.
He causes the clouds to rise over the earth.
He sends the lightning with the rain
and releases the wind from his storehouses.
The whole human race is foolish
and has no knowledge!

Jeremiah 10:12-14 NLT

The LORD takes pleasure in all he has made!

Psalms 104:31 NLT

He watches everyone closely,
examining every person on earth.

Psalm 11:4 NLT

The LORD does whatever pleases him throughout all heavens and earth, and on the seas and their depths.

Psalms 135:6 NLT

The heavens proclaim the glory of God.
The skies display his craftmanship.
Day after day they continue to speak;
night after night they make him known.
They speak without a sound or word;
their voice is never heard.
Yet their message has gone throughout
the earth,
and their words to all the world.

Psalms 19:1-4 NLT

The voice of the LORD echoes above the sea.
The God of glory thunders.

Psalm 29:3 NLT

You are the hope of everyone on earth,
even those who sail on distance seas…
Those who live at the ends of the earth
stand in awe of your wonders.
From where the sun rises to where it sets,
you inspire shouts of joy…
You crown the year with bountiful harvest;
even the hard pathways overflow with
abundance.
The grasslands of the wilderness become a
lush pasture,
and the hillsides blossom with joy.

Psalms 65:5-12 NLT

God arms me with strength,
and he makes my way perfect.

Psalms 18:32 NLT

O God, your ways are holy.
Is there any gods as mighty as you?
You are the God of great wonders!

Psalm 77:13–14 NLT

I know, LORD, that our lives are not our own.
We are not able to plan our own course.

Jeremiah 10:23 NLT

Show me the right path, O LORD;
point out the road for me to follow.
Lead me by your truth and teach me,
for you are the God who saves me.
All day long I put my hope in you.

Psalms 25:4-5 NLT

Lead me in the right path, O LORD,..
Make your way plain for me to follow.

Psalms 5:8 NLT

Put your hope in the LORD.
Travel steadily along his path.

Psalms 37:14 NLT

This is what the LORD says:
"Cursed are those who put their trust
in mere humans, who rely on human strength
and turn their hearts away from the LORD.
They are like stunted shrubs in the desert,
with no hope for the future.
They will live in the barren wilderness,
in an uninhabited salty land.

But blessed are those who trust in the LORD
and have made the LORD their hope and
confidence.
They are like trees planted along a riverbank,
with roots that reach deep into the water.
Such trees are not bothered by the heat or
worried by long months of drought.
Their leaves stay green,
and they never stop producing fruit.

Jeremiah 17:5-8 NLT

Blessed is the man that walketh not in the
counsel of the ungodly,...
But his delight is in the law of the LORD;
and in his law doth he meditate day and night.
And he shall be like a tree planted by the rivers
of water, that bringeth forth his fruit in
his season; his leaf also shall not wither;
and whatsoever he doeth shall prosper.

Psalms 1:1-3 KJV

The Lord says;
This is my command—be strong and courageous!
Do not be afraid or discouraged.
For the LORD your God is with you
wherever you go.

Joshua 1:9 NLT

"When you go through deep waters,
I will be with you.
When you go through rivers of difficulty,
you will not drown.
When you walk through the fire of oppression,
you will not be burned up,
the flames will not consume you.
For I am the LORD, your God, the Holy One."

Isaiah 43:2-3 NLT

Don't be afraid, for I am with you.
Don't be discouraged, for I am your God.
I will strengthen you and help you.
I will hold you up with my victorious right hand.

Isaiah 41:10 NLT

"I, yes I, am the one who comforts you.
So why are you afraid of mere humans,
who wither like the grass and disappear?
Yet you have forgotten the LORD,
your Creator,
the one who stretched out the sky like a
canopy and laid the foundations of the earth.
Will you remain in constant dread of
human oppressors?"

Isaiah 51:12-13 NLT

When I am afraid, I will put my trust in you.
I praise God for what he has promised.
I trust in God, so why should I be afraid?
What can mere mortals do to me?

Psalm 56:3-4 NLT

The LORD is the strength of my life;
of whom shall I be afraid?

Psalm 27:1 KJV

Though I walk through the vally
of the shadow of death,
I will fear no eveil: for thou art with me.

Psalms 23:4 KJV

This is what the LORD says:
Stop at the crossroads and look around.
Ask for the old, godly way, and walk in it.
Travel its path, and you will find rest for your souls.

Jeremiah 6:16 NLT

A man is a fool to trust himself!
But those who use God's wisdom are safe.

Proverb 28:26 TLB

Those who live in the shelter of the Most High
will find rest in the shadow of the Almighty.
This I declare about the LORD:
He alone is my refuge, my place of safty;
he is my God, and I trust him.
For he will rescue you from every trap
and protect you from deadly disease.
He will cover you with his feathers.
He will shelter you with his wings.
His faithful promises are your armor
and protection.
Do not be afraid of the terrors of the night,
nor the arrow that flies in the day.
Do not dread the disease that stalks
in darkness,
nor the disaster that strikes at midday.
Though a thousand fall at your side,
though ten thousand are dying around you,
these eveils will not touch you.

Psalms 91:1-7 NLT

Your unfailing love,
O LORD, is as vast as the heavens;
your faithfulness reaches beyond the clouds.
Your righteousness is like the mighty
mountains,
your justice like the ocean depths.
You care for people and animals alike,
O LORD. How precious is your unfailing love,
O God! All humanity finds shelter
in the shadow of your wings.
You feed them from the abundance
of your own house,
letting them drink from your river of delights.
For you are the fountain of life,
the light by which we see.

Psalms 36:6-9 NLT

The LORD is my shepherd; I shall not want.
He maketh me to lie down in green pastures:
he leadeth me beside the still waters.
He restoreth my soul: he leadeth me in the
paths of righteousness for his name's sake.

Psalms 23:1-3 KJV

The fear of the LORD is
the beginning of wisdom.

Psalms 111:10 KJV

Take delight in the LORD,
and he will give you your heart's desires.
Commit everything you do to the LORD.
Trust him, and he will help you.
He will make your innocence radiate
like the dawn and the justice of your cause will
shine like the noonday sun.

Psalms 37:4-6 NLT

It is good to give thanks to the LORD,
to sing praises to the Most High.
It is good to proclaim your unfailing love
in the morning,
your faithfulness in the evening, accompanied
by the ten-stringed harp and the melody
of the lyre.
You thrilled me, LORD, with all you have done for me!
I sing for joy because of what you have done.
O LORD, what great works you do!
And how deep are your thoughts.

Psalms 92:1-5 NLT

O LORD my God, I cried to you for help,
and you restored my health.
You brought me up from the grave, O LORD.
You kept me from falling into the pit of death.
Sing to the LORD, all you godly ones!
Praise his holy name.
For his anger lasts only a moment,
but his favor lasts a lifetime!
Weeping may last through the night,
but joy comes with the morning.

Psalms 30:2-5 NLT

As the deer longs for steams of water,
so I long for you.

Psalm 42:1 NLT

I take joy in doing your will, my God.
for your instructions are written
on my heart..

Psalm 40:8 NLT

"I will comfort those who mourn,
bringing words of praise to their lips.
May they have abundant peace,
both near and far."
says the LORD, who heals them.

Isaiah 57:18-19 NLT

"Those who trust in me will never be put to shame."

Isaiah 49:23 NLT

The grass withers and the flowers fade,
but the word of our God stands forever.

Isaiah 40:8 NLT

Our days on earth are like grass;
like wildflowers, bloom and die.
The wind blows, and we are gone—
as though we had never been here.
But the love of the LORD remains forever
with those who fear him.

Psalm 103:15-17 NLT

The LORD *says,*
Look up to the skies above,
and gaze down on the earth below.
        For the skies will disappear like smoke,
        and the earth will wear out like
        a piece of clothing.
        The people of the earth will die like flies,
but my salvation lasts forever.
My righteous rule will never end!

Isaiah 51:6 NLT

The humble will see their God at work
and be glad.
Let all who seek God's help be encouraged.
For the LORD hears the cries of the needy.

Psalm 69:32- 33 NLT

The faithful love of the LORD never ends!
His mercies never cease.
Great is his faithfulness; his mercies begin afresh each morning.
I say to myself, "The LORD is my inheritance; therefore, I will hope in him!"
The LORD is good to those who depend on him, to those search for him.
So it is good to wait quietly for salvation from the LORD.

Lamentations 3:22-26 NLT

The LORD will work out his plans for my life.

Psalms 138:8 NLT

Rest in the LORD,
and wait patiently for him:
fret not thyself because of
him who prospereth in his way.
Psalms 37:7 KJV

He fills my life with good things.
My youth is renewed like the eagle's!

Psalm 103:5 NLT

Even in old age they will still produce fruit;
they will remain vital and green.

Psalms 92:14 NLT

The LORD redeemeth the soul
of his servants: and none of them
that trust in him shall be desolate.

Psalms 34:22 KJV

Surely goodness
and mercy shall follow me
all the days of my life:
and I will dwell in the house
of the LORD for ever.

Psalms 23:6 KJV

The LORD will guide you continually,
giving you water when you are dry
and restoring your strength.
You will be like a well-watered garden,
like an ever-flowing spring.

Isaiah 58:11 NLT

How beautiful on the mountains
are the feet of the messenger
who brings good news,
the news of peace and salvation.

Isaiah 52:7 NLT

Teach us to realize the brevity of life, so that we may grow in wisdom.

Psalm 90: 12 NLT

The Lord says;
"Though your sins are like scarlet,
I will make them as white as snow."

Isaiah 1:18 NLT

I—yes, I alone—will blot out your sins
for my own sake
and will never think of them again.

Isaiah 43:25 NLT

I long to obey your commandment.
Renew my life with your goodness.

Psalm 119:40 NLT

Let all those that put their trust in thee rejoice:
let them ever shout for joy,
because thou defendest them:
let them also that love thy name
be joyful in thee.

Psalm 5:11 KJV

The joy of the LORD
is your strength!
Nehemiah 8:10 KJV

If I had not confessed the sin in my heart,
the LORD would not have listened.
But God listen!
He paid attention to my prayer.
Praise God, who did not ignore my prayer
or withdraw his unfailing love from me.

Psalm 66:18-20 NLT

The LORD is close to all who call on him,
yes, to all who call on him in truth.

Psalm 145:18 NLT

O send out thy light and thy truth:
let them lead me;
let them bring me unto thy holy hill,
and to thy dwelling.
Then will I go unto the alter of God,
unto God my exceeding joy.

Psalms 43:3-4 KJV

Listen to my voice in the morning, LORD.
Each morning I bring my requests to you
and wait expectantly.

Psalms 5:3 NLT

The LORD *says,*
I do not want your scrifice. I want your love.
I don't want your offering.
I want you to know me.

Hosea 6:6 TLB

Giving thanks is a sacrifice that
truly honors me.
If you keep to my path,
I will reveal to you the salvation of God.

Psalm 50:23 NLT

The LORD is the everlasting God,
the Creator of all the earth.
He never grows weak or weary.
No one can measure the depths
of his understanding.
He gives power to the weak
and strength to the powerless.
Even youths will become weak and tired,
and young men will fall in exhaustion.
But those who trust in the LORD
will find new strength.
They will soar high on wings like eagles.
They will run and not grow weary.
They will walk and not faint.

Isaiah 40:28-31 NLT

There truly is a reward for those
who live for God;
Surely there is a God who judges justly
here on earth.

Psalm 58:11 NLT

What joy for those whose strength comes from the LORD.

Psalm 84:5 NLT

I will sing about your power.
Each morning I will sing with joy
about your unfailing love...
O my Strength, to you I sing praises.

Psalms 59:16-17 NLT

You will show me the way of life,
granting me the joy of your presence
and the pleasures of living with you forever.

Psalms 16:11 NLT

With God's help we will do mighty things.

Psalm 60 : 12 NLT

The rain and snow come down from
the heavens and stay on the ground
to water the earth.
They cause the grain to grow,
producing seed for the farmer
and bread for the hungry.
It is the same with my word.
I sent it out, and it always produces fruit.
I will accomplish all I want it to,
and it will prosper everywhere I send it.
You will live in joy and peace.
The mountains and hills will burst into song,
and the trees of the field will clap their hands!

Isaiah 55:10-12 NLT

Everything I plan will come to pass,
for I do whatever I wish...
I have said what I would do,
and I will do it

Isaiah 46:10-11 NLT

"If you look for me wholeheartedly,
you will find me.
I will find by you," says the LORD.

Jeremiah 29:13–14 NLT

Be still, and know that I am God!
Psalms 46:10 NLT
I will give you a new heart,
and I will put a new spirit in you.
Ezekiel 36:26 NLT

You can make many plans,
but the LORD's purpose will prevail.
Proverbs 19:21 NLT
From eternity to eternity
I am God.
No one can snatch anyone
out of my hand.
No one can undo
what I have done.
Isaiah 43:13 NLT

About the Author

On September 1, 2001, at her home in Nice in southern France, Julliena Okah received a powerful and mysterious electrical charge that entered her body and inspired her to paint. Even though she had absolutely no training or interest in painting, she started to paint effortlessly and with enormous speed. This energy persisted and inspired her to produce oil and watercolor paintings, and in just a few months, she had over a hundred paintings. Since then, she has had numerous exhibitions, including five one-woman exhibitions that were written about in the *Miami Herald*. Her oil and watercolor paintings hang in fine art galleries, museums, private collections, and auctions worldwide.

Julliena Okah was born in Japan, studied music in Vienna and art in France, and is recognized as a world-class solo violin virtuoso. She became a headliner with her unique solo violin show on international cruise ships and in theaters around the world. She has performed at famous concert halls, including the great commercial venues in Las Vegas and on numerous TV shows. She traveled throughout the world and lived in fourteen countries. At one time, she lived in India, where she studied Indian philosophies. While living in the United States, she has studied Christianity. After living in New York City and Nice for twenty years, she now lives in Southern California.

All the paintings in this book have been painted by Julliena Okah since that fateful day in 2001. Each painting is given a scriptural setting, which enhances the reader's understanding of God.